Whole Food Diet
The 30 Day Healthy Eating Challenge

Abel Evans
©2016

D1502147

Forward

I would like to thank you for purchase the

"Whole Food Diet:

The 30 day Healthy Eating Challenge" and congratulate you for taking the steps to improve your health and wellbeing.

To say that the whole food diet is life-changing would be an understatement. Following the Whole 30 will allow you take control of your health and the benefits that will spill over to all parts of your life. Of course you can expect to see physical changes like definite weight loss and an increase in stamina and strength, and just generally feeling more comfortable in your own skin.

This book will use a step-wise approach to take you through the Whole 30 and further beyond into the practical application of making healthy and super tasty recipes. The Whole 30 expounds on a practical and sustainable way to nourish our bodies to maintain life long health, physical performance and overall wellness.

As you embark on this health journey, I hope it leads you to a life of pure health bliss and vitality as it has for so many Whole 30 devotees.

Table of Content

Introduction

The prevalence of obesity and chronic diseases of lifestyle

Chapter 1

Introducing and Understanding the 30 Day Whole Food Diet

The 30 Day Whole Food Program Unchained

Give us just 30 days

Chapter 2

Breakfast Recipes:

Veggie Packed Breakfast Frittata

Chorizo Scotch Eggs

Fiesta Breakfast Casserole

Sweet Potato Hash and Eggs

Egg and Veggie Muffins

Spicy Pumpkin Patties

Apple Cinnamon Porridge

Dijon Mushroom and Pork Scramble

Banana Almond Chia Pudding

Coconut Green Smoothie

Chapter 3

Lunch Recipes:

Tuna Salad with Garlic Basil Mayo

Sweet Potato and Zucchini Fritters

Steak and Veggie Kabobs

Asian Lettuce Wraps

Lobster Salad with Citrus Vinaigrette

Zesty Chicken Bites

Green Bean Salad with Walnuts

Avocado Egg Salad

Chipotle Chicken Stuffed Sweet Potatoes

Cream of Mushroom Soup

Chapter 4

Dinner Recipes:

Slow Cooker Chicken and Sweet Potato Stew

Thai Stir Fry

Caribbean Salmon

Zucchini Noodle Sloppy Joe Bowls

Creole Style Pork and Cauliflower "Rice"

Slow Cooker Pot Roast

Brazilian Shrimp Stew

Bean-Free Chili

Chicken and Butternut Squash Mash

Beef and Veggie Shepard's Pie

Chapter 5

Snacks:

Pickled Eggs

Buffalo Style Cashews

Protein Power Balls

Zesty Beef Jerky

Banana Snack Cookies

Two Week Meal Plan

Chapter 6

Recommendations for You to Get the Most Out Of Your 30 Days on Whole Foods

Toxin mystery

A Healthy Hormonal System = A Healthy You!

Take some time out to plan your day

Spend less time on the scale and counting calories

Cultivate healthier life habits

Implementing an exciting exercise regime

Remember...

Why cheating isn't an option

Conclusion

Introduction

The prevalence of obesity and chronic diseases of lifestyle

"Let food be thy medicine and medicine be thy food"

~Hippocrates

So many of us have very poor eating habits without even knowing it; this could be attributed to an eating disorder, but a lot of the time it is purely disordered eating. Is it because we have come to rely on foods that are made in a plant instead of growing as a plant? One thing I know is that, nature never intended for us to eat from a box that has been on a shelf somewhere for over 2 months, which most of us do. So what do we expect when we defy nature? Weight gain and a host of diseases!

When walking down the street or going about your daily activities, what's the most prominent thing that catches your eye? For me, it's the rising number of overweight and obese people and sadly, the kids have not been left behind. Consider the fact that, all these you can see from the outside, what about what's going on in the body that you can't see with your naked eye?

The question to ask ourselves is, what happened? When and why did we all of a sudden become fat?

The answer is actually quite simple, the moment we started stuffing ourselves with processed food! There is a very common phrase in technology that I really like to use in relation health and it goes, '**garbage in garbage out**.' Taking it literally, if you feed your body with pure, healthy, natural and whole food, you are going to be the epitome of health. If on the other hand you are always feeding on sweet, fatty, processed and fast foods, am sorry to say you are going to look and feel like junk.

It's important that you understand that eating junk, fast and processed food is the precursor of the diseases of civilization including obesity.

What does the ever increasing number of overweight and obese people mean for our country and the world in general? There may come a time when the life expectancy will only be forty years due to the rampancy of the diseases of civilization – obesity, diabetes, cancer, heart diseases and the like.

If nothing is done, we will no longer have productive people as most of us are going to be sick in hospitals or waiting to die in peace at home. Can you even begin to imagine how this would impact our economy and let alone that, our wellbeing?

Well, it's not all bad news. The whole foods diet is the embodiment of what nature intended for you to eat – fresh, natural and whole foods. But what does 'whole' really mean? It's not that you need to eat your food whole, rather it means eating food that still looks as it did growing as a plant, or very close to it. In short, food that has not been messed with through processing or only minimally messed with. This is because everything in that whole legume, fruit, nut, seed or veggie has already been perfectly arranged by nature and as we know, **'don't mess with mother nature.'**

It is for this reason that I was inspired to write this book. I won't lie, embarking on the Whole 30 is no child's play. But, if you say this is hard, what will a person battling cancer say?

We are now going to get into the 30 day whole food program. Each chapter is going to build onto the next one with valuable tips that have actually helped many people lose weight, grow strong and enjoy better health within just 30 days and a unique blend of yummy recipes.

All of the information you are about to read has been thoroughly researched by both leading scientists and the humble author to ensure that you get the best results you seek. So let's get started on our mission to make you fit healthy and happy with life!

Chapter 1

Introducing and Understanding the 30 Day Whole Food Diet

"If I could bottle the benefits of a healthy lifestyle in a pill, it would become a blockbuster drug."

— Rajiv Misquitta

Think of the 30 day whole food diet like pushing the 'reset' button with your overall health, relationship with food and your habits.

Our premise is actually quite simple: the food you eat will either impact positively on your health or negatively. There's no gray area, it's either black or white – every bite you take is either nourishing your body or making you fat and sick.

This makes everything so simple, right? You only eat the foods that are going to impact positively on your life.

Hmmm. Actually, it partly is and it partly isn't.

So many things come into play when it comes to making food choices and not just whether the food in question is healthy or not.

Ever wondered why after a nasty break up or a very bad day at work you feel like drowning your sorrows in a whole tub of ice cream or a box of chocolates? This is because food is highly emotional and sweet foods trigger the release of dopamine and serotonin which are the feel good hormones that then try to uplift your mood.

Food is also very sneaky, you could have just come from lunch then on seeing a box of yummy looking donuts on your colleague's desk, and you get super cravings like someone who hasn't eaten for a week!

As if this is not challenging enough to staying on the healthy track, every street corner today has a fast food joint and if the hunger pangs hit you, convincing yourself to wait until you get home and have a healthy meal when all the French fries and burgers seem to be calling you by name can be quite an uphill task.

But wait, we are going to make it easy!

We will start by explaining the whole 30 concept, all the benefits you stand to gain that are backed by scientific research. And we will give you very tasty recipes to help launch you into this program and conclusions that sum up the whole 30 then we will set you out on a journey to rediscover your health.

This program will turn you into an experimental guinea pig, so you can do some introspective work and figure yourself out. By the end of this program, you will have firsthand experience on the effects of healthy and natural foods and less healthy and processed foods.

All these in just 30 days!

The 30 Day Whole Food Program Unchained

As you get ready to embark on the Whole 30 journey, the first thing you need to understand is that your health, weight and overall wellbeing are all determined by what you eat. Everything starts with food!

Certain food groups (like dairy, grains, sugar, legumes and processed foods) could be having a very negative impact on your overall health without you even noticing it. Do you have aches and pains that you can't explain? Are you always in need of recharging your batteries? Have you tried everything to lose weight with no success no matter how hard you try? Do you have a medical condition (such as fertility issues, digestive disorders, skin infections ...) that medication doesn't seem to help with?

All these problems may be directly related to your diet, even what you might consider to be the 'healthy stuff'.

Now, the challenge is, how do you know if these foods are affecting you and how they are affecting you?

The answer is quite simple – strip them from your diet for a whole 30 days!

Cut out all the hormone unbalancing, inflammatory, and psychologically unhealthy and gut disrupting food groups for a month and give your body a fighting chance to recover and heal from all the effect these foods have been causing.

It's time to push the 'reset' button with you systemic inflammation, metabolism and all the downstream effects of the diet choices you've been making.

It's time to learn, once and for all, how your food choices are actually affecting your daily life and your long-term health.

The 30 day whole food diet rules

- Yes: eat natural and real food

Eat tons of fresh vegetables, seafood, some fruit, meat, plenty of good fats from seeds, fruits, nuts, fatty fish like salmon and oils. Eat foods with very few and pronounceable ingredients or better yet, foods with no listed ingredients because they are in their pure and natural form.

- No: foods not to eat for 30 days

Most importantly, here's what to AVOID for the 30 days. Omitting all these foods will help you regain your energy, healthy metabolism and significantly reduce systemic inflammation and help you discover how these foods have been impacting your health, quality of life and fitness.

- Stay away from sugar of all kinds (artificial or natural)
- Don't take any alcohol (not even in your cooking)
- Don't eat any grains or legumes
- Don't eat any dairy
- Don't take any MSG carrageenan or sulfites (check your food labels)
- Don't try to recreate treats, baked foods or junk foods with the approved ingredients – continuing to eat your old and unhealthy foods made using whole 30 approved ingredients by for example making kale chips, is totally missing the point. Remember, these are the same foods that got you into the health trouble you are.

One final rule: you should not take any body measurements or step on the scale for the 30 day duration. This way you will focus on your whole self and not just on the weight aspect.

Exceptions to the rule

The following foods are allowed for your whole 30.

- Fresh fruit juice as a sweetener
- Clarified butter or ghee
- Vinegar
- Certain legumes such as snow peas, green beans and sugar snap peas due to the fact that they are more 'pod' and green matter than 'grain'.
- Salt

Give us just 30 days

Your job during the whole 30 is to focus on making healthy and natural food choices. You don't need to stress about grass-fed, organic, free-range or pasture. Jut figure out how to stick to the 30 day whole food program in any setting, under any amount of stress, around every special circumstance... for 30 days straight. Your only job? Eat healthy food!

If you do this, you are going to:

1. Sleep like an angel

When sugar is out the window and healthy protein and fats are in, you will sleep like a baby without tossing and turning at 2.00 am.

2. Enjoy full-blown and consistent energy

Forget about energy highs and lows like a rollercoaster ride, you are going to have so much energy the energizer bunny will be no match for you.

3. Wake well rested and alert

No need for your morning coffee to give you a jolt. All your batteries will be recharged and you are going to wake up with a beautiful smile and an open heart ready to take on the world.

4. Bid farewell to digestive distress

Forget about tummy rumbles and unending gas. You might have a little discomfort if your previous diet did not feature lots of veggies, but after that, it's smooth sailing all the way.

5. Be clear headed and focused

Forget about the tip-of-the-tongue syndrome and brain fog. You will be more alert than ever.

6. Know the difference between real hunger and emotional appetite

You are well familiar with the mindless eating that happens when you are under emotional stress. This is emotional appetite and it's very junky. As your body gets off the sugar spikes and settles into proper insulin management, your appetite will start diminishing and real hunger – the need for nutritious food, will signal you when to eat.

7. Find new favorite foods

There's so much room on your plate and in your kitchen for new tastes now that all the junk is out and who knows which spices, veggies, fruits and meats will become your new favorites?

8. Discover the fountain of youth

Your hair will be shinier and healthier, your skin will be supple and tighter, you will have shed some of the extra pounds. You are going to love it!

These are just a tip of the iceberg, give it a try and you are going to discover a whole world of benefits, you'll never want to look back!

Chapter 2

Breakfast Recipes

"The doctor of the future will no longer treat the human frame with drugs, but rather will cure and prevent disease with nutrition."

~Thomas Edison

Veggie Packed Breakfast Frittata

Serves: 2

Serving Size: ½ a frittata

INGREDIENTS

½ a red onion, thinly sliced

1 carrot, peeled and shredded

½ a red bell pepper, thinly sliced

5-6 cherry tomatoes, halved

2 kale leaves, destemmed and thinly sliced

5 eggs

Freshly ground black pepper

Coconut oil for the pan

Instructions:

- Preheat oven to 350 degrees Fahrenheit.
- Heat the coconut oil, over medium-high heat, in an 8-9", oven-safe pan or cast iron skillet.
- Add all your veggies to the pan and cook for 3-5 minutes, until browned and softened.
- While the veggies cook, whisk the eggs until frothy. Season with freshly ground black pepper.
- Slowly add the eggs to the pan. Reduce heat to medium-low and cook for 5-7 minutes, until the eggs begin to set.

- Transfer the pan into the preheated oven and bake for 10 minutes. Until the eggs are cooked through and golden brown on top.
- Slice the frittata and serve!

To maximize the benefit of a vegetable rich diet, it's important to eat a variety of colors and this veggie packed frittata does just that. It's important to eat a variety of colors to ensure that you're getting a broad range of nutrients.

Chorizo Scotch Eggs

Serves: 3

Serving Size: 2 eggs

INGREDIENTS

12 ounce packages of chorizo sausage

12 ounce package of ground pork

1 jalapeno, seeded and diced

Handful of fresh cilantro, roughly chopped

6 hardboiled eggs

Instructions:

- Preheat oven to 375 degrees Fahrenheit.
- Combine all of the ingredients except for the eggs in a large bowl and mix well with your hands. Divide the mixture into 6 equal pieces.
- To wrap the eggs: Lay a piece of plastic wrap down on your work surface. Take one portion of the pork mixture and flatten it out onto the plastic wrap. Place a hardboiled egg in the middle and lift the plastic wrap, wrapping the egg in the sausage mixture. Repeat for all eggs.
- Place eggs on a baking sheet and bake for 30 minutes, until sausage is cooked through.
- Can be served warm or cool.

Scotch eggs originated in London and eventually made their way over to the U.S. These portable, flavor-packed snacks are perfect on the go.

Fiesta Breakfast Casserole

Serves: 5

Serving Size: 1 slice

INGREDIENTS

1 pound of ground beef, cooked

10 eggs

½ cup Pico de Gallo

1 cup baby spinach

¼ cup sliced black olives

Freshly ground black pepper

Instructions:

- Preheat oven to 350 degrees Fahrenheit. Prepare a 9" glass pie plate with non-stick spray.
- Whisk the eggs until frothy. Season with salt and pepper.
- Layer the cooked ground beef, Pico de Gallo, and spinach in the pie plate.
- Slowly pour the eggs over the top.
- Top with black olives.
- Bake for 30 minutes, until firm in the middle.
- Slice into 5 pieces and serve.

This savory breakfast casserole is easy to throw together, packed with protein, and extremely versatile. Try swapping out the ground beef for ground chicken or the Pico de Gallo for salsa Verde.

Sweet Potato Hash and Eggs

Serves: 2

Serving Size: 2 eggs with hash

INGREDIENTS

1 large sweet potato

¼ teaspoon garlic powder

¼ teaspoon onion powder

½ teaspoon dried parsley

½ teaspoon sea salt

½ teaspoon freshly ground pepper

2 tablespoons coconut oil

4 large eggs

Instructions:

- Peel the sweet potato and shred in your food processor or by hand.
- Toss with the spices in a large bowl.
- Heat the coconut oil in a large, cast iron skillet over medium-high heat.
- Add the hash to the pan and toss for about a minute. Cover, lower heat to medium, and let the sweet potatoes cook for 5-7 minutes. Stirring frequently.
- Plate the hash on two plates.
- Cook the eggs to your desired doneness (additional oil may be needed).
- Top the hash with eggs and enjoy!

Not only are sweet potatoes delicious, but they are loaded with vitamin A, vitamin C, potassium, and dietary fiber, making it no surprise that they rank high on the healthiest foods list.

Egg and Veggie Muffins

Serves: 12

Serving Size: 1 muffin

INGREDIENTS

1 tablespoon olive oil

2 poblano peppers, deseeded and chopped

1 small red onion, chopped

4 cups baby spinach

6 slices of prosciutto, cut in half

12 eggs

½ teaspoon salt

½ teaspoon pepper

Instructions:

- Preheat oven to 350 degrees Fahrenheit.
- Prepare a cupcake or muffin tin by brushing each cavity with olive oil.
- Line each with a slice of prosciutto.
- Heat the olive oil in a skillet over medium-high heat. Sauté the onions and peppers until soft. Add the spinach and cook until wilted. Divide the vegetable mixture evenly throughout the muffin tin.
- Whisk the eggs until frothy. Season with salt and pepper. Pour the egg mixture into the muffin tin.
- Bake for 15-20 minutes, or until the eggs are set.
- Allow to cool slightly before removing from the

muffin tin with a spoon or butter knife.
- Wrap in plastic wrap and store in the refrigerator or freezer for an easy breakfast on the go.

Make a batch or two of these egg and veggie muffins during your meal prep and you'll have them for a quick, grab and go breakfast all week long. They also freeze exceptionally well.

Spicy Pumpkin Patties

Serves: 8

Serving Size: 2 patties

INGREDIENTS

4 cups pumpkin puree

½ cup kale, chopped

½ cup almond meal

1 tablespoon chia seeds

1 tablespoon sesame seeds

2 eggs, lightly beaten

1 teaspoon sea salt

1 teaspoon pepper

1 teaspoon crushed red pepper

½ teaspoon cumin

1 teaspoon turmeric

1 tablespoon coconut oil

Instructions:
- Preheat oven to 350 degrees Fahrenheit.
- Heat the coconut oil in a large pan over medium-high heat. Cook the kale until crispy.
- In a medium bowl, mix the pumpkin puree with the almond meal, chia seed and sesame seeds. Stir in the

spices.

- Fold the eggs and cooked kale into the pumpkin mixture.
- Drop heaping tablespoons of the pumpkin mixture onto a baking sheet that has been sprayed with non-stick spray.
- Bake for 30 minutes, or until the patties are firm and golden brown.
- Serve warm.

The pumpkin in this savory breakfast is high in fiber, while the eggs provide protein, both of which help to keep your appetite at bay.

Apple Cinnamon Porridge

Serves: 4

Serving Size: 6 ounces

INGREDIENTS

½ cup whole cashews

½ cup whole almonds

¼ cup walnuts

1/3 cup unsweetened coconut flakes

1 large, ripe banana

1 tablespoon coconut oil

1 medium apple, chopped

¼ teaspoon nutmeg

1 teaspoon cinnamon

1 teaspoon vanilla extract

1 (14 ounce can) coconut milk

Instructions:

- Add the nuts and coconut flakes to a medium bowl. Cover with water and soak 7-8 hours or overnight.
- Drain the soaked nuts/coconut and rinse well. Add to a food processor along with the banana.
- Pulse the mixture until a fine meal forms. Scraping down the sides, as needed.

- Add the coconut oil to a saucepan over medium heat. Add the chopped apple, cinnamon, and nutmeg. Cook until softened.
- Stir in the coconut milk and vanilla extract. Then add the nut mixture.
- Bring to a gentle simmer and allow to cook for 5 minutes, or until thick and creamy.
- Ladle into bowls and top with a splash of almond milk.

Heart healthy nuts take the place of grains in this warming breakfast. Nuts are a good source of unsaturated fats, which have been shown to help lower cholesterol levels.

Dijon Mushroom and Pork Scramble

Serves: 4

Serving Size: About 1 cup

INGREDIENTS

1 pound ground pork

8 ounces mushrooms, sliced

1 onion, chopped

½ teaspoon salt

½ teaspoon pepper

½ teaspoon dried basil

½ teaspoon dried oregano

2 tablespoons Dijon mustard (non-alcoholic option)

Instructions:

- Heat the olive oil in a large skillet over medium-high heat. Add the mushrooms and cook for about 3-4 minutes.
- Add the onion and season with salt and pepper. Cook another 3-4 minutes, until the onions are translucent.
- Push the veggies to the sides of the pan and add the ground pork.
- Brown the pork and season with the basil and oregano. Once the pork is cooked, incorporate the

mushrooms and onions.
- Stir in the Dijon mustard and mix well.
- Serve and enjoy!

For thousands of years, mushrooms have been celebrated as a powerful source for nutrients. They are a good source of B vitamins, which play an important role in the nervous system. They also contain high amounts of selenium, a mineral that is important to the immune system.

Banana Almond Chia Pudding

Serves: 4

Serving Size: About 1 cup

INGREDIENTS

2 (14 ounce cans) coconut milk

¼ cup chia seeds

2 ripe bananas, sliced

½ cup toasted almonds, sliced

Instructions:

- Open both cans of coconut milk and pour into a medium bowl. Add the chia seeds and mix thoroughly. Cover and refrigerate overnight.
- By morning, the coconut/chia mixture should have thickened significantly.
- Spoon into small bowls and top with sliced bananas and toasted almonds.
- Serve immediately.

Chia seeds are loaded with antioxidants whose job is to fight the production of free radicals, which damage the molecules in cells and contribute to diseases like cancer. Chia seeds take on a gelatinous texture once soaked in liquid, turning a simple can of coconut milk into a rich and creamy pudding like magic.

Coconut Green Smoothie

Serves: 1

Serving Size: 8 ounces

INGREDIENTS

1 cup coconut milk

½ banana, frozen

Handful of baby spinach

½ avocado

Coconut water to thin to desired consistency

Instructions:

- Place the ingredients, in order listed, in a high speed blender.
- Blend until smooth and creamy. Adding coconut water to thin if needed.

With health benefits that include weight management, protection from cardiovascular disease, and enhancing the absorption of nutrients to the body, avocados are a true super food.

Chapter 3

Lunch Recipes

Tuna Salad with Garlic Basil Mayo

Serves: 2

Serving Size: 6 ounces

INGREDIENTS

2 (6 ounce) cans Albacore tuna in water

½ cup garlic basil mayo (recipe below)

1 teaspoon mustard

¼ cup bell pepper, minced

Dash of paprika

Bib lettuce leaves to serve on

Garlic Basil Mayo:

1 egg, room temperature

2 tablespoons apple cider vinegar

½ teaspoon ground mustard

1 clove of garlic

¼ teaspoon salt

½ teaspoon dried basil

1 cup olive oil

Instructions:

- For the mayo: Add all ingredients except for the olive oil to a small food processor or blender. Blend for about a minute then slowly drizzle the olive oil in. Let blend until fully incorporated and smooth. Refrigerate.
- Blend all of the salad ingredients in a small bowl.
- Scoop onto lettuce leaves and sprinkle with paprika.

Albacore tuna is a great source of omega-3 fatty acids. Specifically, DHA, which helps to protect against heart disease, lowers cholesterol, and may help slow Alzheimer's.

Sweet Potato and Zucchini Fritters

Serves: 2

Serving Size: 2 fritters

INGREDIENTS

1 cup shredded zucchini

1 cup shredded sweet potato

1 egg, lightly beaten

1 tablespoon coconut flour

½ teaspoon dried parsley

¼ teaspoon cumin

½ teaspoon garlic powder

Sea salt and freshly ground pepper to taste

2 tablespoons olive oil

Instructions:

- Begin by placing the zucchini in a clean dish towel or paper towels and squeezing some of the excess water from it. This will help it to brown easily.
- Combine the zucchini with the shredded sweet potato and egg. Mix well.
- In a small bowl, mix the coconut flour and spices together. Add to the zucchini mixture and mix well.
- Heat the olive oil in a large skillet over medium-high heat.
- Divide the mixture into 4 equal portions and drop

into the pan, pressing down until about ½" thick. Cook until golden and crisp, flip and cook the opposite side.

- Remove to a plate lined with paper towels and season with additional salt and pepper, if desired.
- Serve warm.

Sweet potatoes contain high amounts of fiber, potassium, and several vitamins, especially vitamin A. And while they do contain carbs and natural sugar, they have minimal effects on blood sugar levels because of their high fiber content.

Steak and Veggie Kebabs

Serves: 4-6

Serving Size: 2 kebabs (1 steak, 1 veggie)

INGREDIENTS

For the marinade:

1 small, red onion

5 cloves of garlic

1 teaspoon orange zest

¼ cup fresh orange juice

¼ cup olive oil

2 tablespoons tomato paste

1 tablespoon fresh rosemary

1 teaspoon sea salt

1 teaspoon pepper

For the kebabs:

2 pounds sirloin steak, cut into 2" pieces

1 zucchini, cut into 1" thick rounds

1 yellow squash, cut into 1" thick rounds

1 green pepper, cut into chunks

1 red pepper, cut into chunks

1 red onion, cut into chunks

Instructions:

- Prepare the marinade: Place all the marinade ingredients into a food processor or blender and blend until smooth. Reserve about ¼ cup for the vegetables.
- Place the sirloin pieces in a bowl and cover with the marinade. Mix well. Refrigerate for at least 4 hours, preferably overnight.
- About 30 minutes before grilling, toss the vegetables with the reserved marinade.
- Remove the beef from the marinade and thread onto skewers. Do the same with the veggies.
- Heat the grill to medium and place skewers on the grill. Cook for 10-12 minutes, turning every couple of minutes to ensure evening cooking. Remove from the grill once the veggies are tender and the steak is cooked to desired doneness.
- Serve immediately or remove from skewers and store in airtight containers for future lunches.

Red meat is a rich source of vitamin B12. Deficiency in this vitamin can result in everything from neurological disorders to cardiovascular disease. It also contains heme iron, a form of iron that is easily absorbed into the body unlike the non-heme iron in plant based foods.

Asian Lettuce Wraps

Serves: 4

Serving Size: 2-3 lettuce wraps

INGREDIENTS

1 pound ground pork

1 pound mushrooms, thinly sliced

1 onion, chopped

3 cloves of garlic, minced

2 cups broccoli slaw

2 green onions, sliced

handful of cilantro, chopped

2 tablespoons apple cider vinegar

2 tablespoons fish sauce

2 tablespoons coconut aminos

2 tablespoons coconut oil

Sea salt and pepper to taste

Bibb or green leaf lettuce to serve

Instructions:

- In a large skillet, over medium-high heat, cook the onions, garlic, and mushrooms in the coconut oil until tender and browned. Season with salt and

pepper.
- Add the ground meat and cook until the no longer pink. Stir in the apple cider vinegar, fish sauce, and soy sauce.
- Once the meat has cooked, lower heat to medium-low and add the broccoli slaw, green onions, and cilantro. Allow the broccoli slaw to soften a bit.
- To serve, scoop the mixture into lettuce cups and enjoy!

Everybody's first choice for lean protein is usually chicken, but pork can be an excellent source of protein and fat in a healthy diet, just be sure to choose lean cuts, or in this case, lean ground pork.

Lobster Salad with Citrus Vinaigrette

Serves: 4

Serving Size: 1 salad

INGREDIENTS

1 pound of lobster meat (can substitute crab meat)

2 avocados, peeled and sliced

1 fennel bulb, thinly sliced

2 oranges, segmented, juices reserved

2 grapefruits, segmented, juices reserved

1 small red onion, diced

½ teaspoon dried thyme

1 teaspoon coriander

½ teaspoon sea salt

½ teaspoon pepper

¼ cup olive oil

4 cups baby spinach

Lemon wedges (garnish)

Instructions:

- In a small bowl, combine the reserved citrus juices and spices. Slowly whisk in the olive oil and mix

until well combined.
- In a medium bowl, toss the fennel, citrus segments, red onion, and baby spinach with enough dressing to coat.
- Divide the mixture among 4 plates and top with the lobster and avocado. Drizzle remaining dressing evenly over the salads.
- Garnish with a couple of lemon wedges and serve!

A single cup of lobster provides a significant amounts of B vitamins which play vital roles in metabolism function and healthy skin maintenance. In addition to being succulent and delicious it's a healthy source of protein.

Zesty Chicken Bites

Serves: 3-4

Serving Size: 6-7 chicken bites

INGREDIENTS

1 pound skinless, boneless chicken breasts

1 egg

¼ cup water

¾ cup almond meal

2 teaspoons Italian seasoning

½ teaspoon cayenne pepper

½ teaspoon paprika

1 teaspoon garlic powder

½ teaspoon crushed red pepper

½ teaspoon chili powder (can be adjusted to desired level of spiciness)

½ teaspoon sea salt

Instructions:

- Preheat oven to 400 degrees. Prepare a metal baking sheet with non-stick spray.

- In a medium bowl combine the almond meal and spices. Mix well.
- In a separate bowl, whisk the egg and water together.
- Cut the chicken into bite sized pieces.
- Drop the chicken into the egg mixture, then transfer to the spice mixture.
- Place the chicken pieces on the prepared baking sheet. Bake for 25-30 minutes, flipping halfway through, until the chicken is crispy and golden brown.
- Serve immediately and store any leftovers in an airtight container in the refrigerator.

Chicken is an important staple in any whole food diet. It's a low-fat form of protein and its versatility cannot be matched. Chicken's high vitamin B6 content has been shown to boost metabolism and keep energy levels high.

Green Bean Salad with Walnuts

Serves: 3-4

Serving Size: About 1 cup

INGREDIENTS

1 pound fresh green beans, washed, ends snipped, and cut in half

1 red onion, chopped

1 cup walnuts, toasted and chopped

Dressing:

2 tablespoons macadamia nut oil

2 tablespoons olive oil

4 tablespoons Dijon mustard (non-alcoholic option)

4 tablespoons balsamic vinegar

¼ teaspoon garlic powder

¼ teaspoon onion powder

¼ teaspoon sea salt

¼ teaspoon black pepper

Instructions:

- Steam green beans until tender. About 5-10 minutes should get them tender, but not mushy.

- When done steaming, submerge in an ice bath to stop the cooking process and retain their color.
- In a large bowl, whisk together the dressing ingredients. Add the chopped red onion and stir.
- Remove the green beans from the water bath and drain.
- Add the beans to the dressing and toss until they are fully coated. This can be made ahead of time and refrigerated for 2-3 days.
- Just before serving, top with the toasted walnuts.

Research shows that walnut consumption may support brain health and improve cell function. The crunchy, earthy flavored nut contains a good amount of heart healthy omega-3 fats and fiber to keep you satiated.

Avocado Egg Salad

Serves: 2

Serving Size: Half the salad (about 6 ounces)

INGREDIENTS

1 ripe avocado

2 hardboiled eggs

1 small tomato

Small bunch of cilantro (optional)

Juice from one lemon

Sea salt and pepper to taste

Instructions:

- Chop the first four ingredients into small pieces.
- Mix together in a bowl and combine with lemon juice and salt and pepper.
- Toss until well combined. Serve atop salad greens, baby spinach, or even inside of a hollowed out tomato for a fancy presentation.

Eggs are a very good source of inexpensive, high quality protein. They also have impressive health credentials. The whites are rich sources of selenium, vitamin D while the yoke contain fat soluble vitamins such as A, D, E and K.

Chipotle Chicken Stuffed Sweet Potatoes

Serves: 2

Serving Size: 1 stuffed potato

INGREDIENTS

2 boneless chicken thighs

2 tablespoons olive oil

1 tablespoon smoked paprika

1-2 teaspoons ground chipotle pepper (depending on desired spiciness)

2 teaspoons garlic salt

1 teaspoon black pepper

2 sweet potatoes

1 cup kale, chopped

½ a red bell pepper, chopped

1 tablespoon olive oil

1 tablespoon lemon juice

Sea salt and pepper to taste

Instructions:

- Bake sweet potatoes at 350 degrees Fahrenheit for about 45 minutes to an hour. Until tender. Set aside. (This can be done well in advance. Just reheat when ready to serve.)

- Heat a large skillet to medium-high. Coat the boneless chicken thighs in the 2 tablespoons olive oil and sprinkle with smoked paprika, chipotle, garlic salt, and pepper.

- Grill for 5-10 minutes per side (depending on the size). Set aside to rest.

- Chop the kale and red pepper and add to a bowl. Whisk the olive oil, lemon juice, and salt and pepper together in a small bowl. Add to the kale and massage in, to soften the kale.

- Finely chop the cooked chicken and add to the kale mixture.

- To assemble, slice the sweet potato lengthwise and mash the insides slightly. Scoop the chicken/kale mixture into the middle of each sweet potato.

- Serve immediately or store in an airtight container in the refrigerator.

The kale and chicken stuffing for the sweet potatoes is a great item to make ahead and have on hand for easy lunches. Bake off a tray of sweet potatoes while you've got that going, and your set for the week!

Cream of Mushroom Soup

Serves: 4

Serving Size: 8 ounces

INGREDIENTS

4 cups homemade beef or chicken broth

4 cups cremini or white button mushrooms, sliced

2 shallots, diced

1 yellow onion, diced

6-8 cloves garlic, minced

2 cups coconut milk (canned)

2 tablespoons coconut aminos

¼ cup coconut oil

3 teaspoons thyme

1 teaspoon sea salt

1 teaspoon black pepper

½ cup flat leaf parsley, chopped (to garnish)

Instructions:

- In a large stock pot over medium-high heat, sauté the onions, shallots, and garlic in the coconut oil until translucent.
- Add the mushrooms and continue sautéing until the

mushrooms begin to soften.

- Season with the thyme, salt, and pepper.
- Stir in the broth and coconut aminos. Bring to a simmer. Reduce heat to low and cook for 30-35 minutes.
- Add the coconut milk and cook for an additional 5 minutes. Remove from heat.
- Using an immersion blender, or working in small batches with a regular blender, puree the soup until smooth and creamy.
- Top with chopped parsley and serve!

Homemade broth has anti-inflammatory and gut healing properties as well as being high in proteins, healthy fats, and minerals. The simplest way to make your own is to keep a large, zip top bag in the freezer to add vegetable scraps and bones to (such as chicken and beef). Once full, place in a stock pot, cover with water, simmer all day and strain. Now you have a delicious, nutrient rich broth to add to soups such as this one!

Chapter 4

Dinner Recipes

One cannot think well, love well, sleep well, if one has not dined well
- Virginia Woolf

Slow Cooker Chicken and Sweet Potato Stew

Serves: 4-6

Serving Size: About 8 ounces

INGREDIENTS

1 pound boneless, skinless chicken breasts

1 yellow onion, diced

3 carrots, peeled and diced

1 large sweet potato, peeled and diced

4 cloves of garlic, minced

2 cups homemade chicken broth

1 can tomato paste

3 tablespoons balsamic vinegar

2 teaspoons whole grain mustard

2 bay leaves

2 cups baby spinach

Sea salt and pepper to taste

Instructions:

- Cut chicken breasts into chunks and add to the pot of your slow cooker.
- Add the onion, carrots, sweet potato, garlic, chicken

broth, tomato paste, balsamic vinegar, mustard, and bay leaves. Stir to combine. Season with salt and pepper.

- Place slow cooker on high for 4-5 hours or low for 6-8 hours.
- An hour before serving, add the spinach and mix well.
- Serve and enjoy! Store any leftovers in an airtight container in the refrigerator or freezer.

The joy of slow cookers! Just dump everything in first thing in the morning and dinner is taken care of! This hearty stew makes a satisfying meal on a cold night.

Thai Stir Fry

Serves: 4

Serving Size: About 8 ounces

INGREDIENTS

Marinade:

1 shallot, minced

2 cloves garlic, minced

½ cup water

½ cup orange juice

1/3 cup coconut aminos

1/3 cup coconut oil

4 green onion, sliced

1" piece of ginger, grated

1 teaspoon vinegar

Salt and pepper to taste

1 pound boneless, skinless chicken breasts, cubed

½ cup broccoli florets

1 (8 ounce package) mushrooms, sliced

2 carrots, shredded

2 zucchini, spiralized (or made into ribbons with a

vegetable peeler)

½ yellow onion, sliced

2 tablespoons coconut oil

Instructions:

- Whisk the marinade ingredients together in a small bowl until well combined. Place the chicken in a separate bowl and cover with half the marinade.
- Heat the coconut oil in a skillet over medium heat. Cook the mushrooms until lightly browned. Add the sliced onion and broccoli and cook until tender.
- Remove from skillet and set aside.
- Add the chicken to the skillet and cook about 10-15 minutes. Toss in the zucchini noodles and shredded carrots. Cook until the zucchini noodles are tender, about 2-3 minutes.
- Return the mushrooms, onion, and broccoli to the pan and stir in the remainder of the marinade.
- Cook and stir until simmering and heated through.
- Serve and enjoy!

If you don't have a spiralizer for the zucchini, you can use a vegetable peeler to make long ribbons, or just chop the zucchini into half-moon shapes. You can also swap the zucchini for yellow squash or spaghetti squash.

Caribbean Salmon

Serves: 4

Serving Size: 4-6 ounces of salmon

INGREDIENTS

1 ½ to 2 pounds of wild salmon filets

3 tablespoons coconut oil, melted

1 clove garlic, minced

1 teaspoon sea salt

1 teaspoon paprika

½ teaspoon black pepper

½ teaspoon oregano

½ teaspoon cumin

½ teaspoon onion powder

½ teaspoon chili powder

¼ teaspoon thyme

Mango Salsa:

1 large, ripe mango, diced

1 avocado, diced

¼ cup diced tomatoes

¼ cup diced red onion

¼ cup cilantro, diced

1 jalapeno, seeded and diced

Juice of ½ a lime

½ teaspoon salt

Instructions:

- Combine the salsa ingredients in a bowl and mix well. Refrigerate until ready to serve.
- Preheat a grill pan or cast iron skillet over medium-high heat. Combine all of the spices in a small bowl. Mix well.
- Coat the salmon filets with the melted coconut oil and rub with the spice mixture.
- Place the salmon filets in the pan, skin side down and cover. Cook for about 3 minutes. Carefully flip the salmon, reduce heat to low, and cover. Cook for about 5 minutes or until the salmon has turned opaque.
- To serve, place on a bed of greens and spoon the mango salsa on top. Enjoy!

Mangoes have been shown to contain antioxidant compounds that protect against colon, breast, and prostate cancers. They also contain high amounts of vitamin C which promotes a healthy immune system.

Zucchini Noodle Sloppy Joe Bowls

Serves: 4

Serving Size:

INGREDIENTS

2 tablespoons coconut oil

1 red bell pepper, diced

1 yellow onion, diced

1 teaspoon salt

1 teaspoon garlic powder

1 pound ground beef

¾ cup homemade ketchup (recipe below)

¼ cup coconut aminos

2 tablespoons tomato paste

2 large zucchinis, spiralized

Instructions:

- Heat the coconut oil in a large skillet over medium-high heat.
- Sauté the pepper and onion in the coconut oil. Cook for about 5 minutes, until they start to soften and onions start to become translucent.
- Sprinkle with salt and garlic powder and stir in.
- Add the beef and break it up with a spatula. Cook until browned.

- Add the ketchup, coconut aminos, and tomato paste. Stir to combine.
- Let cook on low for at least 10 minutes. The longer it cooks the more the flavors will develop.
- Serve over zucchini noodles that have been steamed in the microwave to soften.

Zucchini is an excellent source of dietary fiber and contains high amounts of potassium, an important electrolyte that can help to reduce blood pressure.

Ketchup Recipe:

½ cup dates, pitted and chopped

1 (6 ounce) can tomato paste

1 (14 ounce) can diced tomatoes

2 tablespoons apple cider vinegar

½ cup water

1 teaspoon garlic powder

1 teaspoon salt

½ teaspoon chili powder

- Add all ingredients to a small sauce pan and cook over medium-low heat for 20-30 minutes.
- Puree in a food processor or blender until smooth. Return to saucepan and cook for an additional 10 minutes.
- Store in a glass container in the refrigerator.

Creole Style Pork and "Cauliflower" Rice

Serves: 4

Serving Size: About 8 ounces

INGREDIENTS

2 heads fresh cauliflower

1 pound boneless skinless pork chops, diced

1 yellow onion, diced

½ green pepper, diced

3 tablespoons olive oil

3 cloves garlic, minced

1 teaspoon sea salt

1 teaspoon black pepper

½ teaspoon chili powder

½ teaspoon dried thyme

¼ teaspoon celery seed

Instructions:
- Preheat oven to 425 degrees Fahrenheit.
- Quarter the cauliflower heads and place in a food processor. Pulse several times until the cauliflower resembles rice. You may need to do this in several batches depending on the size of your food processor.

- Place the riced cauliflower in a large mixing bowl. Add the pork, onion, and green pepper. Toss until well combined.
- In a small bowl, combine the olive oil, garlic, and spices. Mix well and pour over the cauliflower. Mix until everything is well coated.
- Divide the rice mixture between two large baking sheets or roasting pans. Bake for 30-35 minutes, stirring halfway through. Cauliflower should be tender and browned in spots.
- Serve and enjoy!

One serving of cauliflower contains 77% of your daily recommended amount vitamin C. It's also a good source of fiber, potassium, and protein, believe it or not!

Slow Cooker Pot Roast

Serves: 6-8

Serving Size: 4-6 ounces of roast, plus vegetables

INGREDIENTS

2 ½ pound chuck roast or London broil

3 cloves of garlic, minced

1 yellow onion, roughly chopped

4-5 celery stalks, roughly chopped

1 cup baby carrots

2 cups homemade beef broth or water

3 tablespoons fresh parsley, chopped

Sea salt and pepper

Instructions:

- Season your roast with salt and pepper.
- Heat a large skillet over medium-high heat. Sear the roast until browned on all sides. Add to the slow cooker.
- Add the vegetables and garlic and cover with beef broth or water. (You may need to add more to ensure that it's covered.)
- Cook on high for 5 hours or low for 8 hours.
- Garnish with fresh parsley and serve!

Try serving this roast over cauliflower mash. Simply

steam a head of cauliflower and puree in a food processor or blender with salt, pepper, and about a tablespoon of olive oil or coconut oil.

Brazilian Shrimp Stew

Serves: 6

Serving Size: About 6-7 shrimp in broth

INGREDIENTS

1 ½ pounds large shrimp, peeled and deveined

¼ cup olive oil

½ yellow onion, chopped

2 cloves garlic, minced

¼ cup roasted red pepper, diced

¼ cup fresh cilantro, chopped

1 (14 ounce) can diced tomatoes with chilies

1 cup coconut milk (canned)

2 tablespoons Sambal Oelek (can be found in the Asian section of your grocery store)

Juice of 1 lime

Sea salt and pepper to taste

Instructions:

- Heat olive in a large saucepan over medium-high heat.
- Sauté the onions until translucent. Add the garlic and roasted red peppers, cook for several minutes.
- Add the tomatoes, shrimp, and cilantro. Simmer

until the shrimp turn opaque.
- Pour in the coconut milk and Sambal Oelek. Lower heat to medium-low and cook until heated through.
- Add the lime juice and season with salt and pepper. Garnish with additional cilantro, if desired.
- Serve immediately.

Shrimp is an excellent source of vitamin B12 which is important for proper brain function. It's also high in omega-3 fatty acids which reduce the risk of cardiovascular disease.

Bean Free Chili

Serves: 6-8

Serving Size: 8 ounces

INGREDIENTS

2 pounds ground beef

2 tablespoons olive oil

1 teaspoon smoked paprika

1 teaspoon sea salt

½ teaspoon chipotle powder

1 yellow onion, diced

2 medium sweet potatoes, peeled and diced

1 medium butternut squash, peeled and diced

1 (14 ounce can) diced tomatoes

2 tablespoons tomato paste

Sea salt and black pepper to taste

½ pound bacon, cooked and crumbled

3 green onions, sliced (garnish)

Fresh cilantro (optional)

Instructions:

- Heat olive in a large stock pot over medium-high

heat.
- Add the ground beef and season with smoked paprika, salt, and chipotle powder. Cook until browned.
- Stir in the onion, sweet potato, and butternut squash. Mix well.
- Add the tomatoes, tomato paste, and beef broth. Season with salt and pepper.
- Reduce heat to medium, cover, and cook for 45 minutes to an hour, stirring every so often.
- The chili is ready once the sweet potatoes and butternut squash are tender.
- Top with sliced green onion and fresh cilantro. Serve!

Beans are excluded from this whole foods diet because they aren't a dense protein source and contain 2-3 times the amount of carbohydrates than protein. They also contain high amounts of phytates which bind to minerals, rendering them unavailable to our bodies.

Chicken and Butternut Mash

Serves: 2

Serving Size: 1 crock/ramekin

INGREDIENTS

2 boneless, skinless chicken breasts

1 medium butternut squash, cut in half and seeded

Coarse sea salt and freshly ground black pepper

Juice of one orange

6 cups baby spinach

½ cup toasted hazelnuts, chopped

¼ cup coconut milk (canned)

Instructions:

- Preheat oven to 350 degrees Fahrenheit.
- Season the butternut squash halves and chicken breasts with salt and pepper. Place the squash halves face down in a large baking dish along with the chicken breasts.
- Pour the orange juice over the chicken and cover the pan with foil. Bake for 30-35 minutes until the squash is fork tender. Set aside to cool slightly.
- In a medium pan, sauté the spinach until just wilted.
- Shred the cooked chicken and add to a large bowl. Using a spoon, scoop out the flesh of the butternut squash. Add in the spinach, toasted hazelnuts, and coconut milk. Gently fold until well combined.

- Divide the mixture between 2 oven safe crocks or large ramekins.
- Place under the broiler for 1-2 minutes until golden brown on top.
- Serve and enjoy!

Winter squashes, such as butternut, are a great source of vitamin A, which supports the immune system. Just one serving contains more than 100% of the daily recommended amount of vitamin A.

Beef and Veggie Shepard's Pie

Serves: 4

Serving Size: ¼ of pie

INGREDIENTS

1 yellow onion, chopped

1 (8 ounce package) mushrooms, sliced

1 pound ground beef

2 tablespoons olive oil

2 tablespoons tomato paste

1 teaspoon mustard powder

½ teaspoon sea salt

½ teaspoon black pepper

¼ teaspoon coriander

¼ teaspoon cloves

¼ teaspoon cinnamon

¼ cup water

1 rutabaga, peeled and chopped

1 cup Brussels sprouts, quartered

¼ cup sliced almonds, toasted

1 large head cauliflower

2 tablespoons olive oil

1 teaspoon Dijon mustard (non-alcoholic potion)

Sea salt and pepper to taste

Fresh parsley, chopped (garnish)

Instructions:
- Heat the olive oil in a large skillet over medium-high heat. Add the mushrooms and cook until golden brown. Add the onion and continue to cook until the onions are translucent.
- Add the ground beef and cook until browned.
- In a small bowl, mix together the tomato paste, water, and spices. Pour the mixture over the beef and mix well.
- Transfer the mixture to an oven safe dish (8x8" works well)
- Cut the cauliflower into small florets and add to a saucepan with about 1 cup of water. Cover and steam until the cauliflower is tender.
- In the pan used to cook the ground beef, sauté the Brussels sprouts and rutabaga until tender. Once cooked, layer them on top of the meat mixture. Top with toasted almonds.
- Add the steamed cauliflower, olive oil and Dijon mustard to a food processor or high speed blender. Season with salt and pepper. Blend until smooth and creamy.
- Gently spread the cauliflower mash over the casserole. Drizzle with a bit of olive oil and place under the broiler for 2-3 minutes, until a golden crust forms. (Watch carefully as not to burn.)
- Garnish with fresh chopped parsley and serve!

Shepard's pie is a comfort food that originated in the United Kingdom and Ireland. It's typically a meat pie topped with mashed potatoes, but we swap out the potatoes for cauliflower mash in our version, lowering the carbs and increasing the protein.

Chapter 5

Snacks

Pickled Eggs

Serves: 12

Serving Size: 1 egg

INGREDIENTS

12 large hard boiled eggs

1 red onion, sliced

Fresh dill, about 5-6 sprigs

1 teaspoon mustard seeds

2 cloves of garlic, halved

1 ½ cups apple cider vinegar

½ cup water

2 teaspoons sea salt

Instructions:
- Place eggs in a large, clean jar.
- In a medium saucepan over high heat, bring the remaining ingredients to boil. Reduce heat to medium-low and allow to simmer for 5-7 minutes.

- Pour the mixture into the jar of eggs. If the eggs are not fully submerged, add water.
- Cover and refrigerate for 2-3 weeks.
- Enjoy your pickled snack! These keep well in the refrigerator for several weeks.

These pickled eggs make an excellent afternoon snack, no prepping required. Just one egg contains an abundance of high quality protein, healthy fats, and various vitamins and nutrients.

Buffalo Style Cashews

Serves: 6-8

Serving Size: About ¼ cup

INGREDIENTS

2 cups raw cashews

¾ cup Frank's Red Hot sauce (or other Whole30 approved hot sauce)

1/3 cup avocado oil (or olive oil)

½ teaspoon garlic powder

¼ teaspoon turmeric

Instructions:

- Mix the wet ingredients in a bowl and stir in the seasonings.
- Add cashews to the bowl and mix well, making sure the cashews are completely coated.
- Soak cashews in the hot sauce mixture for 2-4 hours.
- Preheat oven to 325 degrees Fahrenheit.
- Spread the cashews onto a baking sheet and bake for 35-35 minutes. Turning every 10-15 minutes.
- Allow to cool and serve. Store in an airtight container.

Cashews are packed with energy, free radical fighting antioxidants, minerals and are rich in heart healthy fats. These Buffalo cashews are a spicy, crunchy, and delicious snack to have on hand.

Protein Power Balls

Serves: 6

Serving Size: 2 balls

INGREDIENTS

1 cup natural almond butter

1/3 cup coconut cream*

4-5 medjool dates, pitted

½ cup sunflower seeds

*Refrigerate a can of full-fat coconut milk overnight. In the morning, the cream will have risen to the top.

Instructions:

- Blend all ingredients together in a food processor or blender.
- Scoop tablespoon size dollops onto a cookie sheet lined with parchment paper. (A cookie scoop works well for this.)
- Refrigerate at least 30 minutes, until firm.
- Store in an airtight container in the fridge.

Almond butter has a much better nutritional profile than peanut butter as well as a delectable taste. It's an ideal source of protein and heart healthy fats.

Zesty Beef Jerky

Serves: 8

Serving Size: 3-4 pieces

INGREDIENTS

1 London Broil (about 2 pounds), trimmed of all fat

½ cup apple juice

2 tablespoons sea salt

2 teaspoons garlic powder

1 teaspoon black pepper

1 tablespoon crushed red pepper

1 teaspoon coriander

1 teaspoon allspice

2 teaspoons lime juice

Instructions:

- Thinly slice the London Broil, against the grain, into strips.
- Combine the remaining ingredients in a large bowl. Mix well. Add the meat to the bowl, cover, and refrigerate overnight.
- Preheat oven to 250 degrees Fahrenheit.
- Lay the jerky strips onto metal baking pans. Place in the oven and cook for about 6 hours, flipping once halfway through.
- Jerky is done once all moisture has baked out.

- Store in an airtight container.

Trying to find store bought beef jerky that isn't laden with sugar is quite a feat. This beef jerky contains no added sugar, is loaded with protein, and doesn't need to be kept cold, making it a perfectly portable snack.

Banana Snack Cookies

Serves: 12

Serving Size: 2 cookies

INGREDIENTS

2 ripe bananas, mashed

½ cup natural almond butter

1 large egg

½ teaspoon vanilla extract

½ teaspoon baking soda

¼ teaspoon salt

2 teaspoons cinnamon

½ cup unsweetened shredded coconut

½ cup raw pecan pieces

½ hemp hearts

½ cup flax meal

Instructions:
- Preheat oven to 350 degrees Fahrenheit.
- Combine all ingredients until well blended.
- Drop by tablespoons onto a baking sheet lined with parchment paper. (A cookie scoop works well also.)
- Bake for 10-12 minutes until golden brown and firm.
- Enjoy!

Fiber, potassium, vitamin C, bananas have it all! These snack cookies will provide a boost of energy and help to sustain your blood sugar levels.

Two Week Meal Plan

Meal Plan – Week One			
	Monday	**Tuesday**	**Wednesday**
Breakfast	Apple Cinnamon Porridge	Coconut Green Smoothie	Fiesta Breakfast Casserole
Lunch	Steak and Veggie Kebabs	Zesty Chicken Bites	Tuna Salad with Garlic Basil Mayo
Dinner	Bean-Free Chili	Beef and Veggie Shepard's Pie	Zucchini Noodle Sloppy Joe Bowls
Thursday	**Friday**	**Saturday**	**Sunday**
Egg and Veggie Muffins	Veggie Packed Breakfast Frittata	Spicy Pumpkin Patties	Chorizo Scotch Eggs
Asian Lettuce Wraps	Lobster Salad with Citrus Vinaigrette	Chipotle Chicken Stuffed Sweet Potatoes	Sweet Potato and Zucchini Fritters
Chicken and Butternut Squash Mash	Thai Stir Fry	Caribbean Salmon	Creole Style Pork and Cauliflower "Rice"

Meal Plan – Week Two			
	Monday	**Tuesday**	**Wednesday**
Breakfast	Banana Almond Chia Pudding	Sweet Potato Hash and Eggs	Apple Cinnamon Porridge
Lunch	Green Bean Salad with Walnuts	Avocado Egg Salad	Cream of Mushroom Soup
Dinner	Slow Cooker Pot Roast	Slow Cooker Chicken and Sweet Potato Stew	Brazilian Shrimp Stew

Thursday	**Friday**	**Saturday**	**Sunday**
Dijon Mushroom and Pork Scramble	Fiesta Breakfast Casserole	Chorizo Scotch Eggs	Coconut Green Smoothie
Lobster Salad with Citrus Vinaigrette	Chipotle Chicken Stuffed Sweet Potatoes	Tuna Salad with Garlic Basil Mayo	Avocado Egg Salad
Zucchini Noodle Sloppy Joe Bowls	Bean-Free Chili	Beef and Veggie Shepard's Pie	Caribbean Salmon

Chapter 6

Recommendations for You to Get the Most Out Of Your 30 Days on Whole Foods

"He who takes medicine and neglects to diet wastes the skill of his doctors."

~Chinese Proverb

What's the norm?

Wouldn't you know if certain food groups were sapping away your health? Not necessarily. Say you are allergic to a cat that likes to sit on your bedroom window every morning, you wake up with a stuffed nose, eyes are a little bit itchy and teary and you have a slight headache.

But day after day, exposed to the same cat allergy...you start getting used to those feelings and they become your new normal. You no longer notice the stuffed nose, itchy and teary eyes and slight headache, because that's how you feel every morning.

Now you go on a vacation somewhere where there are no cats and the first morning you wake up you have no stuffed nose, your eyes are clear and bright and you have no headache. You feel awesome – and on returning home you are now acutely aware of how terrible that cat makes you feel and you don't allow it to sit on your window anymore..

That's what the whole 30 does for you – remove all potential dietary triggers so you can be truly aware of what your health and life in general would be like without them.

Toxin mystery

Our modern fast-paces life continues to advance in speed and heaven knows for how long we are going to keep up. We are surrounded by convenience everywhere we turn – from instant processed foods to microwaves to electronics. And yet, while everything has gained momentum, one thing remains: our human bodies and nature need balance!

Living on the fast lane can upset the balance that is so necessary for our health and overall wellbeing... and this manifests as toxic overload.

Toxins lodge in your soft tissues, cells, muscle and hugely overwhelm your immune system.

We have been seeing this imbalance and toxic overload in the form of sky rocketing rates of diabetes, obesity, cancer, infertility, heart diseases, allergies, autism and so many more.

So, what can we do?

While it's virtually impossible to avoid all toxins that come with our modern way of living, we have the power to restore balance in our bodies through the whole 30!

But, where do these toxins come from?

- Beauty and cosmetic products
- Processed foods

- Household products such as detergents
- Drugs, including tobacco
- Contaminated air
- Contaminated water or water treated with chlorine

A healthy and natural diet, such as the whole 30 and simple lifestyle changes such as using natural and organic cosmetic and household products can limit your exposure to toxins and drastically improve your health.

With a few tweaks in your daily habits, you can live in the modern world and still balance your health, energy and longevity.

A Healthy Hormonal System = A Healthy You!

The whole 30 good food standards state that the food you eat should elicit a healthy hormonal response in your body.

The hormonal system is like a beautifully constructed web of different hormonal reactions that in turn propel some other actions which are influenced by factors in your food choices, lifestyle choices, and health and stress levels.

The hormonal system chemical courier service in your body. Imagine your hormones needing clear instructions to arrive at their destination. Whatever message they receive is exactly how they react.

Hormones like cortisol, insulin, estrogen, ghrelin. Leptin, testosterone and serotonin among other hormones are all affected by what you eat, your weight, sleeping habits, health history and how you manage stress.

We all want a healthy and normal appetite, stable blood sugar levels, a healthy sex drive, ability to manage stress well and a healthy thyroid. But, let's be real – this is easier said than done.

While you may not be able to control all your hormonal responses, you can at least do your best to take care of your hormonal system.

Here are some simple dietary and lifestyle choices to balance and take care of your hormonal system.

1. Take some time out to plan your day

Before you start on your plan, it's important to realize that you don't have to do everything at once or in the same day, scheduling your week over the weekend will allow you to handle your work, customize your whole

30 meal plan, do a work out and relax, all within 24 hours.

You can also take a few minutes every evening to go through tomorrow's program to ensure that all the meals are in check, your workout, meditation and sleep time are in check and you still have some time to relax.

Remember, failure to plan is planning to fail!

2. Spend less time on the scale and counting calories

The 30 day whole food program is so much more than losing weight. To focus on how you are faring on the weighing scale and spending every extra minute counting your calories will make you miss out on the lifelong benefits and dramatic health changes that the whole 30 has to offer.

So, as a rule of thumb, no stepping on the weighing scale for the 30 day duration, no analyzing body fat or taking any other comparative body measurements and certainly, no counting calories!

However, we encourage you to weigh yourself before starting the program and right after the 30 days so you can see the real tangible results of your health efforts and the results of ditching all the inflammatory foods.

3. Cultivate healthier life habits

If you look at all the amazing things your body can accomplish, there is no question about the fact that your body is a temple. But, so many are the times when you treat like a wood shed instead. How so? Have you ever eaten an entire box of pizza by yourself within minutes?

Well, cultivating healthier habits is the best way to honor your body and to get the maximum benefits of the 30 day whole food program.

In addition to eating fresh, natural and whole foods, get enough sleep – at least 7 hours, go for massages, practice square breathing and other breathing exercises, be one with nature by going outdoors for meditation and relaxation, drink fresh spring waters, take good care of your skin, teeth and bones by going for regular check-ups, etc.

4. Implementing an exciting exercise regime

Exercising doesn't necessarily meaning going for a morning run or hitting the gym for weight exercises. Exercise is what you make it and it should resonate with your greatest passion. Do you love dancing? Sign up for dance fitness classes. Are you more of a spiritual person? Yoga fitness classes will work perfectly for you.

Are you an outdoorsy person? Going for a run in the great outdoors, a hike or rock climbing will suit you perfectly...

If exercise for you feels like a life sentence, then clearly you are doing the wrong exercise. Look deeper within you and determine what you love doing most then go for a fitness routine that's as close to your passion as possible. This way, you will have a blast as you lose all the extra pounds and this will also serve as a great de-stressor.

Remember...

The better you aim for a balanced lifestyle and food program, manage your stress, take care of your blood sugar levels, the better of your hormones will function. The reason for this is because all of these things propel off of the other, so emphasizing on natural, unprocessed food, getting adequate sleep, finding the perfect exercise regimen for you are some of the most positive and influential things that you have control over and that you can make right for the sake of your health.

Why cheating isn't an option

The only way the whole 30 is going to work for you is if you give it the full 30 days: no slips, 'special occasions' and most importantly, NO CHEATS! This is not tough love at play, okay, maybe a little but this is a fact born out of experience and science.

You only need such a small amount of any of the inflammatory foods to break your whole healing cycle – one lick of the spoon mixing the batter, a splash of milk in your morning coffee, one bite of pizza within the 30 days and you have broken the 'reset' button, meaning you have to start all over again from Day 1.

Don't even consider the possibility of cheating or a slip. Unless you physically trip and your face landed on a box of cookies, there is no 'slip.' You make a choice to eat something unhealthy so, don't put it like you had an accident. Commit to the 30 days and don't give yourself an excuse to fail before you even start.

Consider this, if you decide you only want to 'cheat' on one day on your new healthy way of life when confronted with a cake from a box topped with canned frosting that your coworker left in the breakroom you will surely experience headache, bloating, weight gain and fatigue. All are things you remember but don't miss.

You have to commit to the 30 day whole food program, exactly as is. Anything less and you are selling yourself, and your potential health results, short!

Conclusion

"To insure good health: eat lightly, breathe deeply, live moderately, cultivate cheerfulness, and maintain an interest in life."

~William Londen

Thank you again for purchasing this book!

I hope this book was able to help you to open your eyes and see that there is indeed a deep food problem that is slowing you down and making your life miserable day by day. The important thing is that you are now in the know and have all the arsenal to fight off all your unhealthy habits in favor of a clean, healthy and vibrant life.

The next step is to get into the program so you can have firsthand experience of all the benefits we have spoken about in the book. Most importantly, we want you to take part. We need you to take this seriously and see all the amazing results in even unexpected areas.

Even if you don't believe that the 30 day whole food program will make a significant change in your life, if you are willing to sacrifice 30 short days, just do it. It's that important and we trust in it that much!

The 30 day whole food program changed our lives and we want it to change and improve your life as well!

Finally, if you feel that you have received any value from this book, then I'd like to ask if you would be kind enough to leave a review on Amazon to share your positive experience with other readers. It'd be greatly appreciated!

Below you will find some of my other Best Selling books on Amazon.

The Ketogenic Diet: The 50 BEST Low Carb Recipes That Burn Fat Fast Plus One Full Month Meal Plan

Ketogenic Diet: Fat Bombs: 28 Low Carb, High Fat Nutritious Desserts and Snacks for Weight Loss

WILD DIET: The Top 24 Wild Paleo Recipes to Increase Energy and Aid Weight Loss

Anti-Inflammatory Diet: 30 Approved Recipes for Healing, Fighting Inflammation and Enjoying a Pain Free Life

51004234R00060

Made in the USA
Lexington, KY
08 April 2016